Career Perspectives

Interviews with Blind and Visually Impaired Professionals

Compiled by Marie Attmore
Introduction by William F. Gallagher

⅌B American Foundation for the Blind
New York

es: Interviews with Blind and Visually Impaired Professionals
is © 1990 by
American Foundation for the Blind
15 West 16th Street
New York, NY 10011

Printed in the United States of America

94 93 92 91 90 5 4 3 2 1

Library of Congress Cataloging-in-Publication Data

Career perspectives: interviews with blind and visually impaired professionals / compiled by Marie Attmore; introduction by William F. Gallagher.
      p.   cm.
   ISBN 0-89128-170-3
   1. Blind--Employment--United States. 2. Visually handicapped--Employment--United States. 3. Blind--United States--Interviews. 4. Visually handicapped--United States--Interviews.   I. Attmore, Marie.
   HV1652.C37 1990
   331.5'91'0973--dc20   90-430
                                                              CIP

Contents

Introduction

CHOOSING A PROFESSION or career; getting the education, skills, and experiences this requires; and finding a company or organization to work for are rites of passage all of us go through. In this, the experiences reported in *Career Perspectives: Interviews with Blind and Visually Impaired Professionals* are hardly unique. Nevertheless, they are noteworthy, for they describe persistence, determination, courage, and a refusal to be cowed that are not encountered every day. They are the stories of how 20 different people, blind or visually impaired, decided on a professional career—often in the face of repeated discouragement—and achieved career success.

Our intentions in developing this book were several. We wanted to demonstrate that blind and visually impaired persons are not limited to working in a few stereotypical jobs and can succeed in professional positions that are demanding and rewarding. We wanted to provide role models for blind and visually impaired persons who might not be aware that other people with visual impairments aspired to and achieved responsible positions and professional status. And we wanted to let blind and visually impaired persons themselves tell how they got where they are and what helped them get there. This they do most eloquently—so much so that I need say no more but will let them speak for themselves.

We at the American Foundation for the Blind believe that *Career Perspectives* will be a particularly valuable resource for newly blinded individuals and blind youngsters and their families, rehabilitation counselors, educators of blind and visually impaired persons, employers, and the general public. We hope that the experiences described in the book suggest new insights and innovative approaches to employment for people with visual impairments. Our thanks go to Dr. Sharon Sacks of

San Jose State University and to Dr. Dean Tuttle of the University of Northern Colorado, who reviewed an early version of the manuscript. And we would most especially like to thank the blind and visually impaired professionals who consented to be interviewed for this book, who provided photographs for it, and who allowed all of us a glimpse into their lives.

William F. Gallagher
President and Executive Director
American Foundation for the Blind

Career
Perspectives

Merilyn Rosenthal

"Prepare to be rejected but be determined to keep on trying."

A blind student seeking a professional career should, according to Merilyn Rosenthal, former deputy assistant counsel to the governor of New Jersey, obtain the highest quality education possible. She adds, "Cultivate contacts, because you'll never know who can be helpful. Present yourself in the best way possible. Prepare to be rejected but be determined to keep on trying."

Recently made administrative practices officer for the New Jersey Commission for the Blind, Rosenthal has been totally blind since childhood. She had congenital glaucoma, and a hemorrhage at age 9 caused the loss of the remaining sight in her right eye. She received a bachelor of arts degree with honors in history from Douglass College of Rutgers, the State University of New Jersey, and a J.D. from Harvard University School of Law. In addition, she worked one summer as a law clerk specializing in civil rights with the U.S. Department of Justice in Washington, DC.

Rosenthal's position with the state of New Jersey was somewhat analogous to that of a corporate counsel. She did not litigate but rather studied and made recommendations on bills and amendments that crossed the governor's desk for signature. In her present job as in-house attorney with the New Jersey Commission, she drafts regulations for programs, monitors proposed legislation, mounts legislative initiatives, and acts as liaison between the commission and the state attorney general's office. She is particularly interested in regulatory issues.

Rosenthal finds a cane useful for travel. In her former job, she used the services of a full-time reader and secretaries for dictation. Adaptive devices in occasional use were a Perkins brailler, a VersaBraille machine, and tape recorders. She is now considering the possibilities of other adaptive equipment, such as the Kurzweil Personal Reader, for her new job.

Rosenthal struggled for five years after graduation to find a job in the law. "The New Jersey Commission for the Blind was excellent in helping me with my education," she says, "setting out a prescribed plan from nursery school on, and making sure I learned braille, typing, and other skills while providing grants for college and law school." Recording for the Blind also was helpful; Rosenthal received its scholastic achievement award while in college. "Once I was educated, though," she reports, "no agency seemed to have a good program for placement, and none could be of help in marketing my skills and finding a job. My biggest problem seemed to be in getting job interviews, perhaps because my résumé mentions awards I'd received as a blind student. I've always believed that a prospective employer should know up front that I have a visual disability."

Peter A. Torpey

"I just needed to find out what worked best for me."

Although his academic training seemed to suggest that he should pursue a teaching career, Peter A. Torpey, research scientist with Xerox Corporation in Webster, New York, is glad that he followed his own desire "to do something in the real world." Torpey, whose sight has progressively declined because of congenital glaucoma, is now able only to distinguish between light and dark and to read print that is greatly enlarged and of high contrast.

Torpey attended the Lavelle School for the Blind in the Bronx, New York, as well as public schools on Long Island. "In retrospect," he says, "I have mixed feelings about the education at a school for the blind, although I don't regret learning braille and social skills. Many of my classmates had been babied too much and seemed to have trouble. Mainstreaming in a regular public school seemed to work better for me because it helped me to learn in a real environment."

Torpey received a bachelor of science degree in physics from Union College in Schenectady, New York, and a doctorate in applied science on a fellowship from the University of Virginia, doing his doctoral dissertation on fluid mechanics. While investigating job possibilities, he considered aeronautical firms but was attracted to the upstate New York area and liked what Xerox could offer.

Although his résumé did not refer to his blindness, most prospective employers agreed to interview him even though they learned of his visual impairment in initial conversations. "The attitude seemed to be that if I had a Ph.D. in a highly specialized field, I must be competent and motivated," he recalls.

Torpey's job with Xerox involves development of new products with a concentration on ink-jet printers. Although he considers his closed-circuit television to be his most useful tool to keep up with scientific journals and other reading, he also has a braille computer and other adaptive devices. He learned cane travel and has experimented with hand-held telescopes and similar aids. He has found materials from Recording for the Blind to be helpful as well.

Torpey regularly runs a 7-minute mile with sighted colleagues. He can see enough to follow stripes on the side of the road and may lightly place a hand on a companion's shoulder for additional security. After an initial reaction to his blindness that may seem uncomfortable, most people accept him for what he is, he says.

Focusing on early influences in his life, Torpey notes, "I was helped by my mother in learning that there are a lot of different ways of doing things. I was also inspired by my father, who had trained as a chemist and mathematician and later served as a detective with the New York City Police Department. In high school, a teacher who was working on his Ph.D. on the side helped me in physics because he could answer complicated questions. All of them showed me that I just needed to find out what worked best for me."

James S. Kambourian

*"**U**ltimately, it's up to the individual and depends on how much drive one has. You have to make your own way."*

It is possible for a visually impaired person to hold almost any professional position, according to James S. Kambourian, senior planner with the Fulton County Department of Parks and Recreation in Atlanta, Georgia. He adds that he believes that the limits of one's self-concept represent the only limitations on how far one can go in a career.

Kambourian is a partial albino whose vision was impaired by a type of nystagmus. He received a bachelor's degree in horticultural science from Virginia Polytechnic Institute and State University and a master of science degree in environmental design from the University of Georgia School of Landscape Architecture. Kambourian worked two years at Clarendon Gardens, a North Carolina nursery, before returning for his master's degree. He then established a private landscape architecture practice before joining Fulton County as a planner-technician. He was promoted to landscape architect and then to senior planner after receiving his state certification as a landscape architect.

Kambourian is able to drive an automobile, thanks to telescopic lenses mounted on his eyeglasses, and uses a magnifying glass to read small print. He is exploring the use of computers and word processors while currently being aided by secretaries and other sighted assistants. He also makes use of recorded books.

The planner finds that his job has changed from an emphasis on drafting to more personal contact work. Kambourian believes he has been able to "dovetail my needs with those of the department." He now uses the services of another draftsman to put his ideas into presentable form and at meetings depends on a "spotter" to identify persons in the audience wishing to ask questions.

"As I attempted to follow my present career," Kambourian recalls, "many people said, 'No, you won't be able to do it.' Even my college professors thought I wasn't pursuing an appropriate path, although they couldn't suggest anything better. In spite of such discouragement, I've been able to develop a satisfying career. I would recommend that any visually impaired person wanting to go into this line of work realize that it's necessary to be knowledgeable about all forms of aid and rehabilitation devices available. Ultimately, though, it's up to the individual and depends on how much drive one has. You have to make your own way."

Mitch Pomerantz

"**I**'m always looking for other challenges. I suppose my sense of motivation has a lot to do with my upbringing."

Although he believes that blindness may have a certain negative effect on job retention and promotion, Mitch Pomerantz also thinks that success frequently may be based on willingness to work within the system. He is a senior personnel analyst with the Los Angeles municipal government.

Pomerantz was born with cataracts and had some usable vision until he was 12 years old. He lost his sight after many surgical attempts to deal with a detached retina and childhood glaucoma. He retains some light perception.

Although he received both bachelor's and master's degrees in political science from the University of Southern California, Pomerantz at first found job possibilities limited. After he worked briefly as a salesman of educational products and as an administrative assistant, he was hired by the city of Los Angeles as an entry-level junior administrative assistant. He became a labor market analyst for the city after two years and later transferred to the position of personnel analyst before being promoted to senior personnel analyst. Pomerantz notes that he found his own jobs because his vocational rehabilitation counselor "seemed more interested in counseling than in helping me go to work. He thought, for example, that my master's studies were a waste of time."

Although he concedes that "there are some positions that it would be difficult for me to be promoted into," Pomerantz adds, "I've been lucky in having been placed in positions that I've been able to do. I have a problem with handicapped folks who want special opportunities. I'm always looking for other challenges. I suppose my sense of motivation has a lot to do with my upbringing. If you're raised to believe you can do anything you want, you can overcome disabilities. Parents need to try to motivate their children, whether they're disabled or not."

Pomerantz learned braille while in elementary school and studied with a resource teacher while in regular junior and senior high school. He says he acquired daily living skills "by fits and starts. My family was influential in my learning of social skills. My mother wasn't about to put up with stereotypical behavior. It also helped to have sighted friends."

While the office where Pomerantz works is in the process of being computerized, he uses the services of a reader six to eight hours a week. He does reports and other papers on a braillewriter, a Versa-Braille machine, and a manual typewriter.

Pomerantz believes professional job opportunities for blind and visually impaired people must be improved. He did not work until after he had completed college and thinks that "a real problem for blind kids today is that they don't have opportunities to work part time and to learn how to function on the job. The blindness community must think in broader terms," he continues. "Although there are thousands of job titles for sighted people, there are only about 20 or 30 that are recognized as being suitable for blind people. The system is made up of an incestuous group of well-intentioned do-gooders who are unimaginative in their thinking and afraid to let clients fail. I wouldn't have found my present position if I'd relied on rehab counselors," he adds. "Perhaps blind people who have had four to six years of higher education should be considered as nondisabled and as capable of competing on equal terms in the sighted world."

Roger J. Marzulla

"You have to work hard and overcome the concerns of others as well as your own fears."

n pursuing a career in the law, a blind person may have to serve as a test case or even as a symbol, according to Roger J. Marzulla, former assistant attorney general in the Land and Natural Resources Division of the U.S. Department of Justice in Washington, DC. "You have to show that you can not just be a lawyer, but a very good lawyer," says Marzulla, now affiliated with the Washington office of Powell, Goldstein, Frazier, and Murphy, a broad-based Atlanta, Georgia, firm that does work in environmental litigation and legislation.

Marzulla, who developed retinitis pigmentosa as a child, had virtually no vision by the time he was in his early 20s. He now can distinguish only between light and dark and uses a cane for traveling.

Marzulla received a bachelor of arts degree in political science from the University of Santa Clara in California and later received a law degree from the same school, graduating magna cum laude and first in his class. After serving as an associate and then as a partner in a San Jose law firm, he and two other lawyers formed their own firm, specializing in trial work, including business and real estate litigation. He recalls that his first days with a private law firm might have been more difficult than they were, had he not already convinced himself and others that he had what it takes to practice in the profession. "Once you first get your foot in the door," he adds, "the rest should be easy if you have confidence in yourself."

Marzulla later became president of the Mountain States Legal Foundation in Denver, Colorado, supervising a national law practice of many attorneys and involved in issues of individual liberties, government regulation, and private property rights. After two years, he joined the Justice Department in Washington, advancing from special litigation counsel in the Land and Natural Resources Division to deputy assistant attorney general. Later he was appointed and confirmed by the Senate in the position of assistant attorney general.

"I always wanted to be a lawyer," Marzulla remembers, describing how, in college and law school, he made the transition from reading print to using sighted readers and taped materials and then learning braille as his eyesight declined. "Reading college texts is quite a bit more complicated for a blind person. It doesn't involve merely sitting down with the book and a reader," he notes. "You have to get the professor to decide on a text ahead of time, find the book, and coordinate the recording of it. Often, because of logistics, you need to split the text into sections and get several readers. Readers are a perennial problem; you learn to hold on to any good ones that you find."

Marzulla is grateful for the assistance of Lions Clubs International and volunteers who helped in taping and brailling materials that he needed as a student but adds: "I didn't seek as much help as I should have early on, mostly because of my own stubbornness. I wasn't willing to commit myself until I absolutely had to do so. I just wanted to postpone the things that go along with blindness. It's definitely harder to learn braille and mobility when you're older, just as it becomes more and more difficult to learn a foreign language as you approach middle age."

Recently, Marzulla has found his talking computer helpful in the performance of his duties. During the latter part of his tenure there, the Justice Department installed its own computer system, AMICUS, which has access to other databases and is useful for word processing, legal research, and work with electronic mail. He also has an assistant who combines reading with other duties. "A big challenge here in Washington has been in learning to get around, especially since I do a fair amount of traveling," he says. "Over the years, I've also learned to develop my powers of memory and to be well organized."

Marzulla believes that the blindness system needs to use networking to a greater degree, "getting the word out to people that law school is doable. At every stage in my education, I was discouraged and was told that I couldn't make it through college or law school." He adds that the American Blind Lawyers Association recently has been helpful in encouraging potential law students who are blind and alerting them to career possibilities. "I'd be the first to admit that you have to work hard and overcome the concerns of others as well as your own fears," he says. "Parents need to be encouraging and supportive, giving the child or young adult the opportunity to develop while realizing that, sooner or later, they must hold their breath and gradually let go. This is difficult with any child, but especially so with a blind child."

Marzulla and his wife, also a lawyer, currently are learning about parenthood firsthand, having recently adopted infant twins, a boy and a girl. "Blind people should have no hesitation about becoming parents," he says. "We split the duties connected with our children, and we're all doing fine."

Elizabeth D. Campbell

*"**D**on't let people's negativity get in your way. Decide what you want to do with your life and fight for it."*

Because she chose journalism as a career, work that requires a person to adapt to many situations, Elizabeth D. Campbell believes she has become more adaptable in all aspects of her life. "I think that I'm ready to go with almost any situation that arises," she notes. Campbell is a feature writer with the *Fort Worth Star-Telegram* in Texas, where she has worked for five years, since shortly after her graduation from Baylor University in Waco, Texas.

Campbell developed retrolental fibroplasia when she was born three months prematurely. She grew up in Omaha, Nebraska, after her birth in Fort Belvoir, Virginia, and attended public schools except in the second and third grade, when she was enrolled in the Nebraska School for the Visually Handicapped in Nebraska City. Her bachelor of arts degree from Baylor includes a double major in Spanish and journalism.

Campbell became interested in newspaper writing as a career after taking an introductory course in journalism while a college sophomore. However, she encountered some resistance to her vocational choice. "The professor in my Baylor reporting class took me aside early," she recalls, "and questioned whether I could do the work since I was blind. That just made me more determined." She completed the requirements for her degree without any major problems and gained experience by writing for the Baylor student newspaper, covering politics, the needs of homeless people, and other topics.

After graduation, Campbell began her job search by writing to newspapers throughout Texas. She had a number of interviews with small papers, where most editors were skeptical about the ability of a blind person to do the work. "They seemed unwilling to go beyond their own stereotypes about blindness," she observes. Finally, editors at the *Star-Telegram* gave her a reporting job on a trial basis. She was told early on that she would have to do all the work expected of a reporter and would also have to learn to use a computer in her writing. As a client of Nebraska Services for the Visually Impaired, Campbell learned to use an Apple computer with a voice synthesizer. Since then, she has switched to an IBM-compatible unit.

Campbell's first reportorial "beat" covering religion soon expanded to include stories for the newspaper's "Metro" section. Not long ago, she was offered a feature-writing position for the "Lifestyle" section, covering everything from flower shows to a typical day in the life of a bakery. "My favorite type of writing is descriptive," she explains, "so I have to be up-front with people I'm interviewing, telling them I'm blind and asking them to be explicit about what they're doing."

If working under a tight deadline, Campbell uses her VersaBraille for taking notes. If she has more time, however, she likes to use a tape recorder for greater accuracy. She usually takes the bus to and from work but finds taking a taxicab or riding with photographer colleagues a more efficient way to get to interview locations. She also does many telephone interviews.

Campbell depends heavily on Startext, a database of wire service articles that includes an encyclopedia updated every 90 days. She says that reading and researching background material is the most difficult and frustrating part of her job, since sighted readers often are difficult to find and expensive to hire.

Campbell learned cane travel techniques after college graduation in a program sponsored by the Texas Commission for the Blind. Her mother and other family members trained her in daily living skills when she was a child. "I think support at home is important for any child," she states, "but especially so for one who's handicapped, although I don't like to use that word. It's great to have a family that believes you can do something." Although she had for the most part positive experiences with agencies in the blindness system, Campbell notes, "When a blind person goes for assistance, I wish that people at agencies would not always assume we're helpless and need to start from ground zero." Nevertheless, in summing up her thoughts, she has this advice for young blind people: "Don't let people's negativity get in your way. Decide what you want to do with your life and fight for it. You will encounter ignorance and need to ask for help. Just remember that everyone—sighted or not—needs help sometimes."

Harry P. McClintock III

"I saw that I had to define a career goal and acquire credentials toward that goal, often while breaking away from traditional role models."

Success for any individual, disabled or not, is a matter of finding the right slot and gaining recognition for particular skills, according to Harry P. McClintock III, compensation analyst in the Employee Compensation and Relations Department of ARCO Oil and Gas Company in Dallas, Texas. Now totally blind, McClintock was injured in a firecracker accident at the age of 9.

the age of 9. Following the loss of his left eye, the sight in his right eye gradually declined because of glaucoma and cataracts despite attempts at surgical correction. He first received rehabilitation training at a camp sponsored by Lions Clubs International of Texas, learning braille and mobility skills. "At first, though, they had me doing little else but stringing beads," he recalls, "and that was a real blow to my self-esteem."

McClintock believes that his years of living with partial vision have enabled him to learn patience and also to develop the ability to adapt and to communicate his needs to others. He has had to demonstrate, he adds, that he can perform most tasks, if often in ways different from the way in which they are usually performed by people with unimpaired sight.

McClintock, who has been with ARCO since 1976, received a bachelor of arts degree from Texas Christian University, Fort Worth, with a double major in history and English and a minor in economics. He has done graduate work in business at the University of Dallas.

Finding a job after college was not an easy matter, he admits, noting, "I beat the sidewalks for quite a while." Even before graduation, he found that employment recruiters visiting the college campus often did not take liberal arts degrees seriously and usually did not know how to determine that certain adaptations could be made to enable a disabled person to perform a job successfully.

"When I went to the Texas Employment Commission," McClintock remembers, "I found a thoroughly dedicated counselor who worked to find a public relations job or similar position with a public utility. She knew that members of my family had worked in the gas industry and that I had an understanding of it. When one utility's personnel director found, though, that I was totally blind, he was very angry about the commission's referral to them, asking why I hadn't been sent to the Lighthouse, 'because they take care of people like that.' At that time, I was ignorant about affirmative action laws."

Eventually, however, McClintock joined ARCO's Public Relations Department, concentrating on government relations and state lobbying efforts in a four-state area. He credits officials at ARCO with taking a personal interest in him and making a concerted effort to find him a position where he could be used most effectively. Since joining the company, he has moved to increasingly more responsible positions in the Engineering as well as the Public Relations Department. As part of his affirmative action duties with the company's employee relations group, he traveled to Alaska's North Slope oil fields.

To perform his job, he makes use of extensive clerical support as well as a cassette recorder, a talking calculator, and a brailler. He is investigating learning to use a personal computer.

McClintock is grateful for his family's insistence that he be mainstreamed in public school, because "that's where I belonged." He adds, "They provided the challenges and got me to think of my future. I saw that I had to focus on as much education and personal development as I could. I saw, too, that I had to define a career goal and acquire credentials toward that goal, often while breaking away from traditional role models."

There were, however, barriers along the way. "I could have used more reality testing in terms of preparing for my career search," McClintock says. "After graduation, I was assigned to a social worker who had no idea of what to do with a college graduate who wasn't trained for a specific job. In addition, a job counselor at the Texas Commission for the Blind told me I had two career options, either to work at the Lighthouse or to sign up for training as a masseur. The approach of another person at the commission was to call prospective employers and ask, 'Do you have a job for a blind person?' I did struggle to find myself and came to believe that the worst stereotyping often occurs within the rehabilitation system itself."

McClintock acknowledges that the family of a blind or visually impaired young person often has a daunting task. "It's difficult for family members to keep their chins up," he says. "They have to take risks and endure discouragement but also keep working with the child and teaching independence. They've got to talk the situation through and get the shame and heartbreak out in the open. If they don't grieve and process the grief, it's almost impossible to open doors."

Doug Martin

"When I was growing up, my dad . . . convinced me that I'd have to sell any prospective employer on what was special about me."

Blind people determined to seek a professional career need to surround themselves with people who motivate them rather than those who merely sympathize, Doug Martin strongly believes. A physicist at the Naval Ocean Systems Center in San Diego, California, Martin holds a bachelor of science degree in physics and psychology from Muskingum College in New Concord, Ohio, and a master's degree in acoustics from Pennsylvania State University. He worked nine years for Naval Ocean Systems in Hawaii before a recent transfer to California.

Blind from birth because of retrolental fibroplasia, Martin says his father was the single most important influence on his decision to become a scientist. An electrical engineer, the elder Martin began teaching his son the elements of science at age 6 and continued to encourage his interest. Martin also credits a sixth-grade teacher who taught him how to use an abacus, which he found much easier to work with than braille for almost all forms of mathematics. In addition, Dr. Claus Jenota, a professor at Penn State, was extremely helpful in Martin's efforts to adapt and modify scientific apparatuses and methods to his particular needs.

Martin's career involves work with acoustics and computer signal processing. He says that he became interested in this field because "sound is my whole life, and acoustics are so often terrible." He believes that his greatest difficulty in college was convincing his professors to verbalize what they were writing on the blackboard. "An equation means nothing to a blind person, who can't see it," he adds. He taped lectures in school and also relied on his memory but notes that he was often frustrated by not being able to find out what textbook had been selected for a course by the instructor far enough in advance to have it brailled. It was also often difficult, he says, to find readers with technical knowledge.

"My dad made me a braille map before I began college so that I could become oriented to the campus," Martin recalls. "Sometimes there were lab experiments that I couldn't do completely on my own; in those cases my lab partners were helpful. But when I set out to do my thesis in graduate school, I was determined that it'd be based completely on my own lab work. I was anxious to give prospective employers confidence that I could do the work."

Martin attended public schools in suburban Cleveland and spent 80 to 90 percent of his time in mainstream classes. He also worked with a braille teacher in a resource room and learned skills related to cane travel, typing, and other daily living activities. In his work he uses braille and a computer terminal with a voice synthesizer and believes that braille terminals with refreshable displays are urgently needed.

"When I was growing up," Martin says, "my dad used to say that a handicapped person in any competitive situation had to be better at everything to be treated as an equal. He convinced me that I'd have to sell any prospective employer on what was special about me."

Marilyn Lutter

"**D**on't assume too much about what a child can't do, or you may impose limitations, both academically and socially."

A blind person seeking a professional career should begin with the best possible academic preparation, according to Marilyn Lutter, director of social services at the Hospital for Sick Children in Washington, DC. She is married to Rudolph Lutter, assistant professor of communications law at the Howard University School of Communications in Washington, whose experiences are also described in this book.

Marilyn Lutter has had Leber's disease, a nonprogressive form of macular degeneration, since birth. She is totally color blind and sensitive to bright lights and has little ability to see detail. A telescope or bioptic mounted on the lenses of her eyeglasses has given her an enhanced ability to focus on objects up to 20 feet away. Like her husband, she was graduated from Overbrook School for the Blind in Philadelphia, although the couple did not meet until later. She graduated first in her class with a bachelor of arts degree in sociology from Wilkes College in Wilkes-Barre, Pennsylvania, and received a master's degree in social work from the University of Pittsburgh.

"At Overbrook," she recalls, "the vocational teachers were especially helpful in assisting me to learn to use my hands efficiently, even though they knew I was pursuing academic areas more strongly. As a residential student, I enjoyed the attention that house parents were able to give me on weekends, when less structured activities were designed to help build individual confidence."

Lutter served as a psychiatric social worker at Retreat State Hospital in the Wilkes-Barre area, was later a social worker at Friendship House in Scranton, Pennsylvania, and then worked as a social worker at Moss Rehabilitation Hospital in Philadelphia. She has held her present position in Washington for close to 10 years.

Lutter attributes her successful career to a good intellectual capacity and a family that made the decision, while she was still in high school, that she needed to prepare to take care of herself while also making a contribution to the world. "My mother was a schoolteacher who valued education," she notes. "She read to me a great deal and, after I'd been at Overbrook and learned braille, let me accompany her to her classroom in a public school. She'd have me demonstrate my braille skills to her sighted pupils, thereby allowing me to build up my confidence while learning to interact with people in the real world. When my father would drive me back to Overbrook after vacations," she adds, "he'd take the time to talk with me and help instill pride and confidence in my abilities."

Although she knew braille when she went on to college, Lutter also had to learn to utilize sighted readers and recorded materials. "I had my hardest time in graduate school," she remembers. "We were required to do our academic work plus 24 hours of field work. It was also the first time that I'd run into the situation where all the books in the library that I needed were on reserve. I really made use of volunteer readers then."

On the job, Lutter depends heavily on her knowledge of braille, uses a tape recorder, and receives other assistance from her secretary and a volunteer reader. She has obtained a talking computer and is finding it helpful in reviewing material.

Lutter says she is concerned that the concept of the "least restrictive environment," or mainstreaming, provided by P.L.94-142, the Education for All Handicapped Children Act of 1975, may be producing undesirable results. "Technology is wonderful," she observes, "but I have real concerns that a significant number of blind students haven't developed braille skills and thus can't really read or write." Her view of being married to another visually impaired person is that "you can learn so much from someone who has been there, someone who understands." Lutter also believes that families of visually impaired young people "can't protect their kids from negative things and disappointments without smothering them. Don't assume too much about what a child can't do, or you may impose limitations, both academically and socially."

Art Schreiber

"Develop any special skills and the confidence to go and do the job."

onvincing people who became blind as adults that "it's not the end of the world, although admittedly it's not always easy" is a personal crusade of Art Schreiber, vice president and general manager of KKOB AM and FM in Albuquerque, New Mexico. Schreiber lost his sight at age 54 because of torn and detached retinas. After 15 eye operations, he retains minimal central vision in one eye and "pinhole" vision in the other.

Schreiber holds a bachelor of arts degree in psychology and Bible philosophy from Westminster College in Pennsylvania and has done graduate work in psychology at Kent State University in Ohio. He began his career in the 1950s, working as a newsman for stations in Ohio, Chicago, Philadelphia, Los Angeles, New York, Minneapolis-St. Paul, and Washington, DC. He was a national correspondent for the Westinghouse network, covering civil rights, manned space flights, and presidential election campaigns, and he also traveled with the Beatles on their first U.S. tour. Schreiber has been in Albuquerque since early in the 1980s. He believes himself nontraditional in having moved from the news side of broadcasting to management, because most managers come up through sales.

Schreiber notes that he had "major concerns about job retention" when he lost his sight but adds that officials of Hubbard Broadcasting, owners of KKOB, "believed I could do it. They knew I'd performed well, as proved by the fact that the station was—and remains—number one in our listening area." Toward his goal of continuing in his position, he learned cane travel and orientation and mobility skills. Although he acquired a VTEK reading machine, he also depends on his secretary to serve as his reader. He uses a talking calculator and hopes to learn braille.

Schreiber serves as chairperson of the New Mexico Commission for the Blind and on some "14 or 15 other boards" in the state. He is president of the New Mexico Broadcasters Association and vice president of HealthNet, an organization that promotes physical fitness. "I've even become a runner, albeit a slow one, after I learned a special track for running," Schreiber notes.

For young visually impaired people contemplating professional careers, Schreiber says, "I offer three bits of counsel. First, learn to accept your blindness. Then, I advise you to get as much training as possible to enable you to perform in society. Finally, I suggest that you develop any special skills and the confidence to go and do the job. We have to change the attitudes of the public about blindness and show that we can be mobile and work at all kinds of jobs."

He adds, "We have to convince ophthalmologists to be more helpful. We've got to work to give blind people more opportunities. Family members should learn to deal with blindness by learning to communicate and by refusing to wait on the blind person. In addition, we blind people need to be vocal about what we need and want."

Charles P. Westpheling

"You'll find it can be done if you want to do it badly enough."

Although he acknowledges that there is no quick or simple way to cope with the onset of blindness in adulthood, Charles P. Westpheling, a stockbroker who lost his sight at age 56, says, "You'll find it can be done if you want to do it badly enough." The broker, who resides and works in Fort Worth, Texas, now has a special interest in older clients and their financial needs. He is 80 years old, extremely vigorous, and has no plans to retire, although he is considering "slowing down."

Westpheling first became aware that his eyesight was declining when he had trouble reading stock market quotations. His difficulty was diagnosed as an inflammation of the optic nerve. He finds that he can still "see a bit," if there is high contrast between dark and light.

A graduate with the West Point class of 1931, Westpheling retired with the rank of colonel after 30 years in the army. Upon his retirement, he decided to go into brokering, a field that had always interested him. He has worked for several firms and has been with his current firm, Eppler, Guerin, and Turner, for 13 years.

When his sight first declined, Westpheling found his job almost impossible to do. With the help of his wife, he developed new ways of doing things and learned braille on his own. He finds that he uses the braille "every day, without fail." The broker found things "tough going" for the first several years and often became discouraged. He had to develop his memory and work aggressively on getting referrals for new accounts. Clients and colleagues were at first unaware of his declining vision because it did not materially change his approach to his work. "I didn't make a point of it," he says, "because I was selling stocks, not blindness." Westpheling recalls one incident a few years ago when a client brought in a stock certificate and asked Westpheling to show him where to sign it: "When I told him I couldn't, he was shocked. He'd had no idea that I was visually impaired."

The broker now is assisted by a sighted reader-secretary and depends on a suction-cup recorder attached to his telephone to discuss orders with clients. He also uses a braille watch, a talking clock, a talking calculator with keys labeled in braille, and a Perkins brailler to keep accounts in braille. He gets around by using a cane.

Westpheling credits the Lighthouse of Fort Worth for help in learning braille and the Texas Commission for the Blind for help in learning cane travel. Currently, he is investigating use of a computer and has ordered a braille-and-speak device that will audibly synthesize words he types in braille and later produce a typewritten printout.

Westpheling recommends that young visually impaired persons seeking a professional career get a college education and learn braille, because "it will be a tremendous help." The stockbroker adds, "Never trade on your handicap. I personally deplore people who are not able to say the word 'blind.'"

Carl Schmitt

"I want to keep the wheels turning and keep organized."

As his sight has gradually declined, Carl Schmitt, principal engineer and president of a Washington, DC, private consulting firm for satellite communications, says he has become extremely aware of what it is to be visually disabled and has worked to find ways to compensate. The engineer's eye problems began in his early adulthood with mysterious eye inflammations and gradual degeneration of sight. Later he developed cone dystrophy and then an atypical form of retinitis pigmentosa. He also has cataracts, has developed tunnel vision, has lost night vision, and is unable to see in bright-light situations.

Schmitt uses a cane for travel and, as his ability to read even large print has declined, has come to depend more and more on a computer, which allows him to control brightness and contrast. He has acquired a scanner that enables him to load almost any page directly onto his computer and an optical character recognition system with a voice output. "I'm a very visually oriented person, so I naturally have hang-ups about giving up the use of my eyes," he notes.

Schmitt received a bachelor of science degree in electrical engineering from Virginia Polytechnic Institute and State University and has done postgraduate work in telecommunications at George Washington University. He has performed varied engineering assignments for COMSAT and other private firms dealing with the U.S. government in communications areas, working on location in Europe, Central America, and the Mideast. He witnessed the first launch of a communications satellite from Cape Kennedy, Florida, in the 1960s. Since becoming a private consultant, he has completed a number of projects for such clients as the National Geographic Society and is also doing work in the area of voice recognition.

Schmitt has received assistance from the Virginia Department for the Visually Handicapped, Volunteers for the Visually Handicapped in Maryland, the Council of Citizens with Low Vision of the American Council of the Blind, and other organizations, learning cane and other skills that will be necessary as his eyesight continues to decline. He also uses volunteer readers and recorded material as much as possible.

When he experienced his greatest loss of vision, between 1983 and 1986, COMSAT, his employer, called in Washington, DC, social service agencies for recommendations on equipment that would allow Schmitt to continue to do his work. He found that he had to find his own devices and appliances, because his social worker was overwhelmed "with too many people and too many families needing help more critically than I did."

When Schmitt could no longer do his work, he suffered "feelings of job loss" but also found it "encouraging and exciting" to explore new areas and continued his education in microcomputers and related areas at Montgomery College in Maryland. "I want to keep the wheels turning and keep organized," he notes. He believes that the blindness system needs to concentrate more efforts on functional vision evaluation, applying evaluations to a person's area of interest and helping to prove to potential employers that suitable ways can be found for a qualified employee to succeed on the job.

Rudolph Lutter

"**E**ven if the odds against achieving a goal are 100 to 1, a person doesn't know where the one chance that will lead to success is located, so he or she should use up all the negative chances to find it and by eliminating them thereby finally succeed."

Rudolph Lutter, assistant professor of communications law at the Howard University School of Communications in Washington, DC, believes that persistence is the most important quality a blind person can exercise in seeking a professional career. He is married to Marilyn Lutter, director of social services at the Hospital for Sick Children in Washington, whose experiences are also described in this book.

Lutter's eyesight began to decline after he was 9 years old because of retinitis pigmentosa and has progressively gotten worse. He now has limited travel vision and uses a cane.

Lutter attended a public grammar school in Philadelphia, where he had difficulty reading and was at first believed to be retarded. When he was finally diagnosed as having retinitis pigmentosa, he transferred to the Overbrook School for the Blind in Philadelphia. He received a bachelor of arts degree from Pennsylvania State University with a major in psychology and a minor in government and a J.D. from the Harvard University School of Law. Lutter credits Delta Gamma sorority members for reading help while he was in college. Although he also used paid readers, he says they often were not as good as volunteers, probably because they were doing it for the money rather than from a sense of commitment.

Because he was heavily involved in extracurricular activities as an undergraduate, Lutter's professors recommended that he pursue a doctoral degree in sociology. He believed, however, that this course of study would confine him to only one career, teaching, whereas studying law would enable him to practice law, teach, or pursue government service.

After graduating from law school, Lutter practiced law briefly in Philadelphia but found it difficult to attract clients. "Nobody wanted to trust a young, blind lawyer with serious matters, especially those involving money," he recalls. He then joined the Federal Communications Commission (FCC) and had attained the rank of senior attorney by the time he left 18 years later to do private consulting. Shortly afterward, he joined the Howard University faculty.

At the FCC, Lutter suggested that he be hired at a lower level, GS-9 rather than GS-11, so that the difference in salary could be used to hire a reading assistant for him. "Later," he notes, "Section 501 of the Rehabilitation Act of 1973 was interpreted as mandating the hiring of readers for blind workers in government agencies, but many of the agencies still do everything they can to get out of this commitment. It continues to be difficult for blind people who work in the government to get readers."

At Howard, Lutter has been aided by Volunteers for the Visually Handicapped, who have put all his textbooks on tape, and by the fact that he has committed much of his highly specialized course material to memory. The university provides a teaching assistant who administers exams and marks papers for him. He considers braille also very important to his career.

As a white person teaching at a university with a majority of black students, Lutter believes he has come to understand the dynamics of prejudice better. "If a blind person—or a black person—is able to do things better than colleagues, this may be unacceptable to the colleagues. In other words, if a minority person appears to be equal or even better, the majority person may feel inadequate or threatened."

Reflecting on his decision to marry another visually impaired person, Lutter says that both he and his wife Marilyn understood the possible pitfalls that can confront a blind couple. "We both were determined, however, that we wanted to spend our lives with someone who understood the frustrations of blindness rather than with someone who would be a nursemaid."

Lutter believes that attending a school for the blind, such as Overbrook, may be preferable to mainstreaming for many visually impaired students. "Often," he adds, "blind students in a mainstream situation aren't truly integrated, especially if they don't have tools such as braille that would enable them to do the work. In addition, few blind students emerge as leaders in public school extracurricular activities the way they do in a special school, where their blindness often becomes an irrelevance.

"Although I was considered a kind of 'Peck's bad boy' at Overbrook, several of my teachers could look beyond my facade and see a potential for success. This was later confirmed for me at Penn State when Milton Eisenhower, the president of the university, insisted that I plan to go to Harvard Law even when that institution's officials were doubtful."

Striving toward goals continues to be important to Lutter. "When I was a student at Overbrook," he remembers, "we called our superintendent 'Percy' because he was always stressing persistence. He told us that even if the odds against achieving a goal are 100 to 1, a person doesn't know where the one chance that will lead to success is located, so he or she should use up all the negative chances to find it and by eliminating them thereby finally succeed."

Steve Hanamura

"**F**ind two or three people who believe in you and make sure they're in your corner at your worst moments."

Contacts made within volunteer organizations can often help a visually impaired person find employment and business prospects, says Steve Hanamura, a management consultant and counselor who maintains his own business in Portland, Oregon. "I believe that the best way to achieve something is to serve, whether among friends, at church, or in the community," he adds.

Although he has been blind from birth because of unknown causes, Hanamura retains some peripheral perception of light and dark. He is a graduate of the California School for the Blind and Oakland Technical High School and holds a bachelor's degree in psychology from Linfield College, McMinnville, Oregon, and a master's degree in counseling from the University of Oregon.

Hanamura was employed at Lane Community College in Eugene, Oregon, as an instructor and counselor for 10 1/2 years and held executive positions with the Oregon State Commission for the Blind for several years. Later, he was a private employee relations contractor for U.S. Bancorp.

Hanamura does not single out one mentor in his background but instead says that various people have inspired and helped him at every stage in his life, beginning with the first person who volunteered to type his college term papers. He has always made it a practice to observe and learn from diverse successful people he has known or noticed, such as Walt Disney and John Wooden, the legendary basketball coach at the University of California in Los Angeles.

Hanamura's current business, which uses the theme "Celebrate Oneness," aims at helping businesses and individuals with leadership development, cross-cultural training, and self-empowerment. He is active in the American Society for Training and Development and has given presentations at conferences.

Hanamura uses both public transportation and volunteer drivers. When traveling, he asks on arrival for orientation around airports and hotels. In his work, he uses both paid and volunteer readers as well as dictating equipment. He is also investigating the use of a VersaBraille machine.

Hanamura believes that, too often, rehabilitation counselors attempt to encourage only technical career goals for their visually impaired clients. He recalls that he was told at one point that vocational counseling, an area in which he later worked for a number of years, was an almost impossible career for a blind person. He also says that not enough emphasis is placed on attaining what he calls a "business mind set," or on becoming focused on a definite career goal.

Hanamura says he is encouraged that job interviewing for blind people appears to have changed for the better in the last 20 years, but he also believes that entry-level jobs are still difficult for visually impaired people to obtain. Institutions of higher education may unintentionally put blind students at a disadvantage by not giving them enough accurate feedback about their strengths and weaknesses, he adds. "Success for anyone, whether visually impaired or not," he says, "requires moxie, persistence, determination, purpose, a good self-image, spiritual beliefs, and a personal resource inventory of technical, fiscal, and human needs. Find two or three people who believe in you," he advises, "and make sure they're in your corner at your worst moments."

Nigel B. Ricards

*"**D**on't let others discourage you. Be persistent and always follow your original goals."*

G etting through school and entering the business world "wasn't all that easy" for Nigel B. Ricards, associate engineer and scientist with IBM in Boca Raton, Florida. Although he concedes that his quest "took a lot of hard work and many difficult times," he adds, "I was helped by being absolutely determined that I was going to be an electrical engineer."

Ricards, born in Trinidad but now a naturalized U.S. citizen, has been totally blind from birth because of an undeveloped optic nerve. He has a minimal amount of light perception.

Ricards attended summer programs for visually impaired people at Florida State University, learning independent living skills and taking two courses prior to formal enrollment. He notes, "I had known since my early high school days that engineering was my career goal. I first got interested when involved with ham radio as a hobby." After receiving a bachelor of science degree in electrical engineering from the University of Florida, Ricards was immediately hired by IBM. While still in school, he worked one summer for a company that developed technical products. He received the national scholastic achievement award of Recording for the Blind from President Ronald Reagan in a ceremony in the White House Rose Garden.

He recalls that, while seeking a job, he worked closely with his university's career resource center, checking frequently to find out which companies were interviewing on campus. One recruiter was "so taken aback" to discover that Ricards was blind that he "didn't know what questions to ask." Another, however, was so favorably impressed that although he had no position to offer at the time of the interview, he remembered Ricards later when he became a recruiter for IBM.

Ricards says that preparation is the key to successful job hunting. "Make sure your résumé is the best it can be," he recommends, "and find out as much as you can about the company that interviews you. Pay close attention to your personal appearance, strive for eye contact, and avoid stereo-

Parental support and being in the right place at the right time have been important elements in her career, Pshon Barrett believes. She is an assistant U.S. attorney based in Jackson, Mississippi, head of a debt collection unit and specializing in civil litigation and bankruptcy.

Blind since birth because of retrolental fibroplasia, Barrett is a graduate of the Mississippi School for the Blind. She credits the school for maintaining a curriculum similar to that of a public school, which she believes gave her a well-rounded academic background and enabled her to go on to university and law school studies. Barrett received a bachelor of arts degree in history from Mississippi

State University and a J.D. from the University of Mississippi School of Law. She served in two summer law clerkships, one in the Mississippi state attorney general's office and another in the U.S. attorney's office in Washington, DC.

Barrett learned various daily living skills, including braille, while attending the Mississippi School for the Blind but received other training on her own with the help of her family. Before acquiring cane travel skills at the Addie McBryde Rehabilitation Center for the Blind, she had used a dog guide for 12 years. Barrett notes that one disadvantage of a residential facility, such as the Mississippi School, is that blind students often have few opportunities to interact with sighted people.

Barrett first became interested in studying law when she was participating in political campaigns as a high school student and college undergraduate. Although she was then interested in a political career and saw law school as an obvious first step, she has since decided not to pursue politics.

As a college senior, Barrett attended a meeting of the American Blind Lawyers Association, an organization in which she now participates regularly. She met a number of people who influenced her choice of law as a career and found Jack Rivers, at that time a U.S. attorney in the Birmingham district, to be particularly helpful and encouraging.

After law school, Barrett worked for a year as an in-house general counsel for a state agency administering the Comprehensive Employment and

Training Act (CETA) program. When she joined the U.S. attorney's office, she worked in the criminal division, prosecuting cases for three years before moving to her present post in the civil division.

Barrett's full-time secretary serves as her reader, driver, and court assistant. Because most legal materials are still not available in forms accessible to a blind person, students from Mississippi College School of Law nearby also perform volunteer reading tasks for her. Barrett uses an Apple IIe computer with speech synthesizer to access JURIS, a U.S. Department of Justice database, and depends on taped and brailled materials as well.

Barrett believes that physical appearance and social skills are of the utmost importance in her job. She has used the services of a wardrobe consultant and uses both braille labels and notes to enable her to match articles of clothing easily.

Although Barrett gives credit to various rehabilitation agencies for helping to finance her college education, she notes that they were of only limited assistance in her search for employment. Agency representatives provided help in filling out forms or securing transportation, but Barrett herself usually made her own inquiries and arranged her own interviews. "As a native Mississippian, I strove to build up contacts even while in school and serving my clerkships," she notes. "From the beginning, my parents instilled in me the attitude that I could do anything I was determined to do. Their goal was for me to be as independent as possible."

Michael Harrell

*"**I**'d rather be frustrated in trying to do something than sit back and let others take care of me."*

Acrucial need of a newly blinded person is having the help of someone familiar with available resources, according to Michael Harrell, director of cardiopulmonary services for Medical Center Hospital in Port Charlotte, Florida. Harrell was blinded at age 27 when the 10-speed bicycle he was riding collided with an automobile. He had previously had extensive surgery for congenital glaucoma.

Prior to the accident, Harrell had received an associate's degree in respiratory therapy from Columbia Union College in Takoma Park, Maryland, and had worked for a year and a half in a West Virginia outpatient clinic for black lung disease. After taking examinations to qualify as a registered repiratory therapist, he had returned to Columbia Union College and had received his bachelor of science degree in respiratory therapy. He had then worked as a full-time respiratory therapist in the intensive care unit of Washington, DC, Adventist Hospital before moving to Florida to become staff respiratory therapist at Medical Center Hospital.

"When I lost my sight, job retention was a major concern," Harrell recalls. "I said to myself, 'Well, flush the old career. What will a blind respiratory therapist do?' I had many worries and didn't know if I'd ever go back to work." He continues: "When I was home after 13 weeks in traction for a broken femur, the director of my department began talking about my returning to work. He didn't even consider the possibility that I'd not be back and believed I had the qualifications to be a good supervisor. Having finished my bachelor's degree helped, and it didn't hurt that I had several years of hands-on experience."

Harrell was back on the job six months after his accident, working first as a staff therapist before being promoted to director of respiratory therapy. He is now responsible for both respiratory therapy and cardiology services.

Harrell uses a closed-circuit television with a voice synthesizer attached to a computer for most of his work. He also is assisted by a secretary and uses taped materials and braille file labels. He has studied braille by correspondence. "When I needed assistance," he notes, "I had to be the aggressor and found the Florida Division of Blind Services on my own. My doctor knew nothing about such help." Harrell believes that there is a great need for a professional support network to help disabled persons contact other professionals in similar job situations.

Harrell finds it easiest to be frank about his blindness with people who may not be familiar with his condition. In daily situations, he confides, getting needed assistance is easier than letting people know tactfully that help is not needed. "I try to play it by ear but sometimes find myself grabbed and dragged across a street when all I need is an elbow to grasp lightly." He adds, "The worst thing a blind person can do is be too quick to be discouraged by what he perceives as his own limitations. Most apparent limitations really aren't. I'd rather be frustrated in trying to do something than sit back and let others take care of me."

William H. McCready

"I'm appalled at the attitude of some . . . of the current generation of blind law students, who are constantly demanding more readers and other services provided without charge by the state. I believe that society should treat us normally while being sensitive to our physical limitations."

blind person who wants to become a lawyer needs to have an aptitude for the law but should also be able to overcome the superficial barriers imposed by society, Judge William H. McCready says. He is judge of the probate and

juvenile court in Iosco County, Michigan, having sat on the bench for 25 years.

McCready lost his sight as a young man when a pistol he was holding discharged, severing his optic nerve. He had completed his army service and was waiting to take an examination to qualify as a state trooper when the accident occurred. Vocational aptitude tests indicated he had the ability for a career as a farmer or a mortician, but he considered both ideas somewhat impractical.

Opting instead to continue his education, McCready received a bachelor of arts degree in social sciences from Michigan State University and an LL.B. from the University of Michigan School of Law. He took a correspondence course in braille while in college, where he met his future wife, a member of a women's honorary society that did volunteer reading for blind students. He attempted to learn cane travel but was given a cane that was too short and never mastered it. He then enrolled in the program of Leader Dogs for the Blind in Rochester, Michigan, and is now using his third dog as a guide.

After he passed the Michigan bar examination, McCready discovered that friends had written in his name on a ballot for justice of the peace. After serving in that position, he ran for the office of county prosecutor, was elected, and served four years. He then ran on a nonpartisan ballot for his current judgeship and has been reelected five times.

In his work, the jurist uses a Royal manual typewriter to rough out his decision after a hearing. The rough draft is then given to a secretary for final typing. He is assisted both by his wife and his secretary, who read necessary printed materials for him, and notes that he has been told that he is "blessed with an excellent memory" for the facts as they appear in a case.

McCready believes that any prospective lawyer, blind or sighted, also needs to have speaking ability, a good grasp of the English language, and an interest in people. Even though he recommends the law as a satisfying career for a young visually impaired person, he is not enchanted by everyone who aspires to be a lawyer. "I'm appalled at the attitude of some members of the current generation of blind law students, who are constantly demanding more readers and other services provided without charge by the state," he says. "I believe that society should treat us normally while being sensitive to our physical limitations."

Timothy T. Fenerty

"You must be overt in discussing limitations while making it clear that one can still be capable."

he primary message the families of visually impaired persons must make clear to them is that having a disability does not make them limited in other ways. This is the opinion of Timothy T. Fenerty, clinical and administrative supervisor at a private psychiatric facility for elderly persons in the Philadelphia area.

Legally blind as the result of albinism, Fenerty can perceive colors and read with enhanced reading glasses. His distance vision is extremely impaired, and he must use telescopic magnifiers to watch television. He is, however, able to travel independently on trains and buses.

Fenerty received a bachelor's degree in psychology from Kenyon College in Gambier, Ohio, and a master's degree in community psychology from Temple University in Philadelphia. After he got his undergraduate degree, he worked two years full time and six years part time in a psychiatric hospital in suburban Philadelphia, assigned to treatment units for crisis intervention, adolescents, and alcoholism. After receiving his master's degree, he became a full-time therapist in a community mental health facility and was later promoted to assistant coordinator and then to program coordinator.

"Early on," Fenerty states, "I had the feeling that I wanted to find out how to relate successfully to others and be helpful to them. I believe that I've been blessed with intelligence, so that I found it easy to do well in school. I did occasionally have to use creativity in problem solving and find new ways to do things that I couldn't do in conventional ways. In grade school, for example, I was allowed to move my desk closer to the blackboard without asking permission, and my teachers tried to make written work clear for me."

In his academic work, Fenerty used some large-print or taped materials. Now, on the job, he may occasionally ask a co-worker to read case reports to him.

Although Fenerty believes that any problems he had with the blindness system were the result of lack of attention to detail by practitioners, he applauds the fact that "federal legislation has required increased emphasis on public accessibility." He cautions families of visually impaired young people to avoid labeling anyone as limited. "You must be overt in discussing limitations while making it clear that one can still be capable," he notes. "Be creative in finding ways to have the person excel to promote self-esteem and socialization."

About the Author

Marie Attmore is a freelance writer and editorial consultant who lives in Oregon. She is the coauthor of *Creative Recreation for Blind and Visually Impaired Adults,* also published by the American Foundation for the Blind.

About the
American Foundation for the Blind

The American Foundation for the Blind (AFB) is a national nonprofit organization that advocates, develops, and provides programs and services to help blind and visually impaired people achieve independence with dignity in all sectors of society.

∞

It is the policy of the American Foundation for the Blind to use in the first printing of its books acid-free paper that meets the ANSI Z39.48 Standard. The infinity symbol that appears above indicates that the paper in this printing meets that standard.